This diary belongs to

_____

who really loves horses!

MY HORSE DIARY for Girls

Rebecca E. Ondov

HARVEST HOUSE PUBLISHERS
EUGENE, OREGON

Cover design by Left Coast Design

Cover photo © KellyJHall / iStock

Backcover author photo and interior photos with an * are copyright © 2014 (or earlier) by Deborah K. Hamilton, Debbie Hamilton Photography, Hamilton, MT. Used by permission. All rights reserved.

Interior photos not marked with an * are copyright © 2014 (or earlier) by Rebecca E. Ondov. Used by permission. All rights reserved.

Published in association with Books & Such Management, 52 Mission Circle, Suite 122, PMB 170, Santa Rosa, CA 95409-5370, www.booksandsuch.com.

MY HORSE DIARY FOR GIRLS

Copyright © 2015 Blazing Ink, Inc.
Published by Harvest House Publishers
Eugene, Oregon 97402
www.harvesthousepublishers.com

ISBN 978-0-7369-6615-3 (pbk.)

Printed in China

15 16 17 18 19 20 21 22 23 24 / RDS-JH / 10 9 8 7 6 5 4 3 2 1

A Note to You

Hi. My name is Rebecca, and I've been horse crazy as long as I can remember. Are you horse crazy too? When I was a young girl I didn't own a horse, so I used to write in my diary about my dream horse. Maybe you're like me and hope to own your very own horse, or maybe you have a horse and love to dream. This diary is the perfect place to write about all of those things.

In these pages I've occasionally posted some questions, pictures, and ideas to help inspire you to journal. Feel free to do this or follow your imagination. Jot down your secret thoughts as well. And why not doodle some pictures of your wildest dreams?

Let's have fun together!

Rebecca Ondov

Rebecca and Czar*

"God can do anything, you know—far more than you could ever imagine or guess or request in your wildest dreams!" (Ephesians 3:20 MSG).

"Horses are gifts from God wrapped in love and tied with His heartstrings as a bow."

(*Rebecca Ondov*, Heavenly Horse Sense)

"God said, 'I command the earth to give life to all kinds of tame animals, wild animals, and reptiles.' And that's what happened. God made every one of them" (Genesis 1:24-25).

Have you ever thought of God as having a huge imagination? Look at all the different-looking horses He created! Why not draw or paste pictures of your dream horses on this page?

"SkySong's big, white blotches looked like clouds, and the dapple black-and-gray made his body look like a stormy sky."

(*Rebecca Ondov,* Heavenly Horse Sense)

Rebecca, SkySong, and Sunrise.*

Did you know that horses use their noses like dogs do? They love to explore the world by sniffing things.

"My friendly horses and mule stretched their necks and gently snuffled five-year-old Cassie from head to toe."

(Rebecca Ondov,
Great Horse Stories for Girls)

"Jesus said, 'Let the children come to me, and don't try to stop them!'" (Matthew 19:14).

"The newborn foal's head wobbled, and it whinnied. My heart leaped. Instantly I wondered, *Lord, does Your heart skip a beat when I speak Your name?*"

(*Rebecca Ondov*, Horse Tales from Heaven)

How would you feel if your dream
horse whinnied when it saw you?

_____

_____

_____

_____

_____

_____

_____

_____

_____

_____

_____

_____

_____

If you could choose your very own horse,
what three things would you look for?

_____

_____

_____

_____

_____

_____

_____

_____

_____

_____

_____

_____

_____

_____

"God chose you out of all the people on Earth as his cherished personal treasure" (Deuteronomy 14:2 MSG).

"Have you ever thought about how exciting it is to be chosen? What if you could *know* deep inside your own heart that you are important and valuable?"

(*Rebecca Ondov*, Great Horse Stories for Girls)

How would God create your dream horse so it would be unique? How about the way He created you—in what ways are you unique?

_____

_____

_____

_____

_____

_____

_____

_____

_____

_____

_____

_____

_____

"The newborn colt wiggled his rear, switched his tail, and slurped. I couldn't take my eyes off of him."

(*Rebecca Ondov*, Heavenly Horse Sense)

"The LORD chose me and gave me a name before I was born" (Isaiah 49:1).

I've named lots of horses and mules, some after their markings, like Star (who had a star on her forehead) and Dusty (who was dust colored). What ideas do you have for names of your dream horses?

_____

_____

_____

_____

_____

_____

_____

_____

_____

_____

"We have been given a wonderful gift from God—
the ability to decide how we'll act and who we'll
become. Through those decisions, we're choosing
what our names will mean."

(*Rebecca Ondov*, Great Horse Stories for Girls)

"I know you well and you are special to me. I know you by name" (Exodus 33:17 MSG).

There are lots of different breeds of horses. Can you list some of them? How did you hear about them? (Type "horse breeds" on the internet to find more breeds.) Why not draw or cut out pictures of different breeds of horses and paste them on these two pages?

Some horses have spots, which vary in looks from faint ones called "dapples" to showy ones. Draw a spotted horse. What would you name it?

There were even horses mentioned in the Bible that had spots (dapples).

_____

_____

_____

_____

_____

_____

_____

"The third chariot was pulled by white horses, and the fourth by spotted gray horses" (Zechariah 6:3).

_____

_____

_____

Have you ever noticed that different breeds
of horses have different body builds, which
make them really good for particular jobs?
Draft horses are often used for pulling wagons
and doing heavy work. Why not look up "draft
horses" and then draw one or two types?

"Nugget was a deep, golden-brown with a reddish-brown mane and tail. He was tall with muscles that bulged in his chest and through his haunches."

(*Rebecca Ondov,* Heavenly Horse Sense)

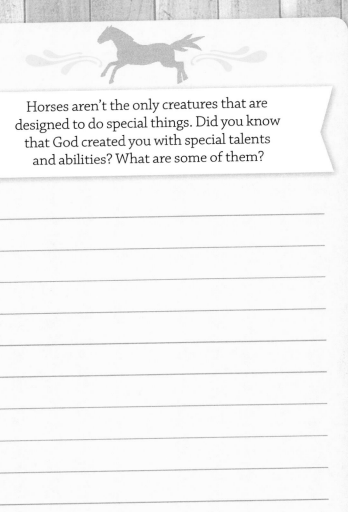

Horses aren't the only creatures that are designed to do special things. Did you know that God created you with special talents and abilities? What are some of them?

_____

_____

_____

_____

_____

_____

_____

_____

_____

_____

_____

_____

_____

_____

What types of things would you like to do with your horse? Trail ride? Barrel race or jump? Ride it in a parade? Or maybe pull a cart? Why not draw a picture (or paste one in) of you doing something fun with your horse?

Did you know there are breeds of horses that were developed to walk quickly and smoothly?

"I rode Dancer down the dirt road, and my body barely rocked side-to-side because her gait was so smooth."

(*Rebecca Ondov*, Great Horse Stories for Girls)

_____

_____

_____

_____

_____

_____

_____

_____

_____

_____

_____

Dancer, Rebecca's Tennessee Walking Horse.

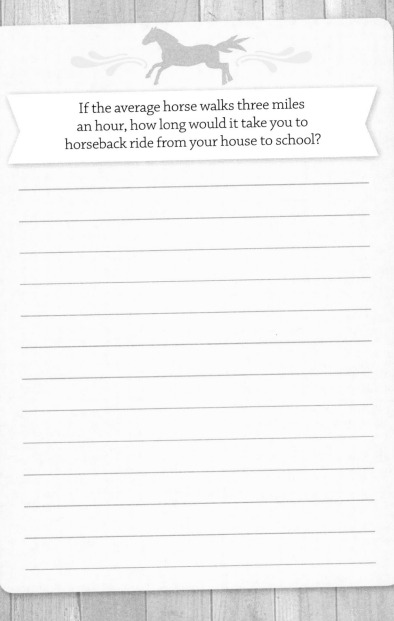

If the average horse walks three miles
an hour, how long would it take you to
horseback ride from your house to school?

What breed of horse do you dream of owning?
What do you like about that breed?

_____

_____

_____

_____

_____

_____

_____

_____

_____

_____

_____

_____

_____

"God made everything with
a place and purpose"
(Proverbs 16:4 MSG).

"The only One who can look inside of you and really know what's going on is God. He sees inside your heart."

(Rebecca Ondov, Great Horse Stories for Girls)

A horse's pedigree shows on which day
the horse was born. What would you
do for your horse on its birthday?

_____

_____

_____

_____

_____

_____

_____

_____

_____

_____

_____

_____

_____

Would you like to raise a baby horse or mule?
What do you think would be your favorite part?

_____

_____

_____

_____

_____

_____

_____

_____

_____

_____

Wind Dancer, my mule
colt, and Czar.

Besides varying colors and breeds, horses have different personalities from each other too. Some are affectionate and love to snuggle.

_____

_____

_____

_____

_____

_____

_____

_____

_____

_____

_____

_____

_____

_____

_____

_____

Dazzle giving me a hug.*

"Create in me a clean heart,
O God" (Psalm 51:10 NLT).

Have you ever thought about having
a horse so gentle that you could fall
asleep on it? What do you think would
happen if you fell asleep on a horse?

_____

_____

_____

_____

_____

_____

_____

_____

_____

_____

_____

_____

"Miles rolled past as Amarillo plodded the mountain trail. My head bobbed. I slouched in the saddle and napped."

(*Rebecca Ondov*, Heavenly Horse Sense)

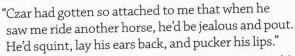

"Czar had gotten so attached to me that when he saw me ride another horse, he'd be jealous and pout. He'd squint, lay his ears back, and pucker his lips."

(*Rebecca Ondov*, Great Horse Stories for Girls)

Have you ever had a relationship with
an animal like I had with Czar?
Imagine what that would be like...

_____

_____

_____

_____

_____

_____

_____

_____

_____

Did you know that God loves you so much that He wants to be your only God?

"Do not worship any other god, for the LORD...is a jealous God" (Exodus 34:14 NIV).

"We must love God with all our heart, mind, and strength" (Mark 12:33).

What kind of personality would you
like your horse to have? Explain why.

_____

_____

_____

_____

_____

_____

_____

_____

_____

_____

_____

_____

_____

If you had a whole day to spend with your dream horse, what would you do? Why not draw pictures of that?

Did you know that most horses enjoy getting brushed?

"Pushing Czar's black mane aside, I brushed his neck with a soft-bristled brush. He closed his eyes and leaned into the brush, enjoying the massage."

(*Rebecca Ondov,* Horse Tales from Heaven)

Rebecca and her dream horse Czar.*

"I gently scratched the filly's haunch. In a few minutes she was wiggling her rear side-to-side like a hula dancer."

(*Rebecca Ondov*, Heavenly Horse Sense)

"Keep on loving one another
as brothers and sisters"
(Hebrews 13:1 NIV).

If you could ask your horse what he or she would like you to do, what do you think he or she would say?

_____

_____

_____

_____

_____

_____

_____

_____

_____

_____

_____

_____

_____

"Friends come and friends go, but a true friend sticks by you like family" (Proverbs 18:24 MSG).

Horses can see really well at night—even when it's pitch-black outside. What do you think it would be like to ride on a rocky, mountain trail—in the dark?

_____

_____

_____

_____

_____

_____

_____

_____

_____

_____

_____

"In the black night, Sunrise, a palomino, trudged up and down the shallow swales along the mountain. I felt like I was riding a roller coaster in slow motion."

(*Rebecca Ondov,* Heavenly Horse Sense)

"The LORD turns my darkness into light" (2 Samuel 22:29 NIV).

Did you know that each horse and mule has its own unique smell or fragrance? Although my horse SkySong smells sour, I still love to bury my nose into the fur on his neck and take a deep breath.

SkySong.*

"To those who are being saved, we are a life-giving perfume" (2 Corinthians 2:16 NLT).

Did you know that some horses like human treats? I heard about one horse that liked ice cream!

"Licking his lips, my horse SkySong stared at my treat. I laughed and said, 'Chocolate chips are bad for horses.' But SkySong ate it anyway!" (P.S. It's better to give horses carrots or apples.)

(*Rebecca Ondov*, Great Horse Stories)

"Dear friend, don't let this
bad example influence you.
Follow only what is good"
(3 John 11 NLT).

Have you ever played music for horses
and watched their reaction? Have you
ever listened to Christian music to
keep from being stressed out?

_____

_____

_____

_____

_____

_____

_____

_____

_____

_____

_____

"The signal on the radio came in clearly and the melodious notes of K-LOVE radio drifted through the barnyard. Instantly Dancer stopped pacing and relaxed."

(*Rebecca Ondov*, Great Horse Stories for Girls)

Dancer.

"Whenever the evil spirit from God bothered Saul, David would play his harp. Saul would relax and feel better, and the evil spirit would go away" (1 Samuel 16:23).

Did you know that horses recognize people from a long way away? Mine even recognize my car and run to greet me.

How would you feel if your dream
horse saw you and came running?

"I blew a shrill whistle. SkySong raced toward me, his black mane and tail flowing. At that moment God spoke to my spirit, 'I'm delighted when you run to me.'"

(Rebecca Ondov, Great Horse Stories)

"I am the holy God, the LORD All-Powerful! Run to me for protection" (Isaiah 8:13-14).

Have you ever heard of this? When baby horses and mules get hurt, sometimes the owners bring them into the house to live for a short period of time until they get well enough to go outside. What would your mom say if you brought a horse into the house?

_____

_____

_____

_____

_____

_____

_____

_____

_____

_____

"The scrambling sounds of tiny hooves scraping up my wooden kitchen floor jarred me awake. The three-day-old, lanky, brown mule foal stood in the kitchen inside a small area I'd fenced off."

(*Rebecca Ondov,* Great Horse Stories)

Have you ever dreamed of getting a horse
as a present? Describe your dream horse.

_____

_____

_____

_____

_____

_____

_____

_____

_____

_____

_____

_____

_____

_____

_____

_____

_____

_____

_____

_____

_____

_____

_____

_____

_____

_____

_____

"Early in the morning, before the sun came up, I snuck into Rahab's stall and wrapped a wide red ribbon around her neck."

(*Rebecca Ondov*, Heavenly Horse Sense)

How do you say "hi" to a horse? One way is with a "horseman's handshake." Sometimes when I do this, their whiskers tickle my hand.

Rebecca and Dazzle, the "horseman's handshake."*

"I walked over to Dancer and extended my hand in the 'horseman's handshake,' which meant that I held my hand close to her nose with my palm facing downward."

(*Rebecca Ondov*, Great Horse Stories for Girls)

Horses make friendships with other horses. Do you have friends who make you feel special? Who are they?

Did you know that Jesus had 12
special disciples who were His friends?
How many can you name?

_____

_____

_____

_____

_____

_____

_____

_____

Jesus wants to be your friend too.
Are you His friend?

_____

_____

> "Dancer and Czar faced each other, nose to nose, their nostrils quivering. Czar's eyes brightened. He arched his tail and shifted his shoulders. Suddenly he looked ten years younger!"

(Rebecca Ondov, Great Horse Stories for Girls)

Wind Dancer, Dancer, Rebecca, and Czar.

What would you (and your horse) do on a
Saturday if your best friend had a horse too?

_____

_____

_____

_____

_____

_____

_____

_____

_____

_____

_____

_____

"My goal with horses and mules is to get to know them so well that I feel like they're part of me. Do you have friends you're so close to that you can almost tell what they're thinking?"

(*Rebecca Ondov*, Great Horse Stories for Girls)

My horses and mules are wonderful friends, but my best friend in the whole universe is Jesus. Is He yours too? If He is, when did you become best friends?

_____

_____

_____

_____

_____

_____

_____

_____

_____

_____

_____

"In herds of wild horses, the 'alpha' or lead mare is the horse that mothers the herd. She's responsible for the herd's overall safety and health."

(Rebecca Ondov, Great Horse Stories for Girls)

_____

_____

_____

_____

_____

_____

_____

_____

_____

_____

_____

_____

"Just like in a horse herd, there are leaders and followers within groups of people. Who are the leaders in your life?"

(*Rebecca Ondov*, Great Horse Stories for Girls)

"I [the living LORD God] will give you a shepherd...He will be your leader, and I will be your God" (Ezekiel 34:23-24).

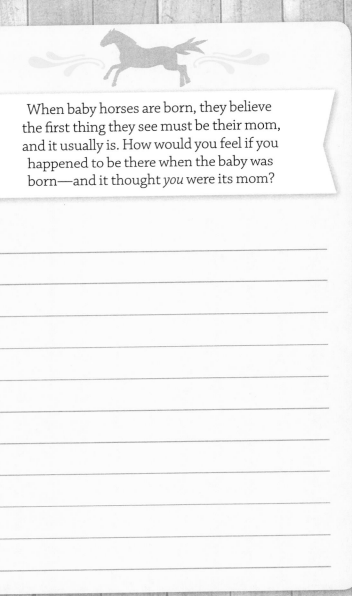

When baby horses are born, they believe the first thing they see must be their mom, and it usually is. How would you feel if you happened to be there when the baby was born—and it thought *you* were its mom?

_____

_____

_____

_____

_____

_____

_____

_____

_____

"The foal fastened its brown eyes on me and batted its long, black eyelashes. Then it whinnied. *Wow, this baby thinks I'm its mom!*"

(*Rebecca Ondov*, Horse Tales from Heaven)

"Keep your eyes on Jesus"
(Hebrews 12:2 MSG).

Is there anything in your life that's
boring? How could you make it fun?

_____

_____

_____

_____

_____

_____

_____

_____

_____

_____

_____

> "My mule colt, Wind Dancer, was using the boring pasture as an opportunity to play the game 'King of the Hill.'"
>
> (*Rebecca Ondov*, Great Horse Stories for Girls)

Wind Dancer having fun.

"We should make the most
of what God gives" (Ecclesi-
astes 5:19 MSG).

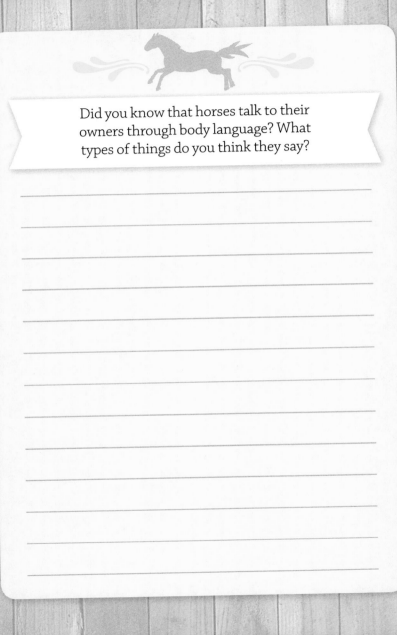

Did you know that horses talk to their owners through body language? What types of things do you think they say?

_____

_____

_____

_____

_____

_____

_____

_____

_____

_____

"My red mare lifted her top lip up so that her white teeth showed. Over and over she waved her head into the sky and waggled her lip. It was her way of saying 'Thank you' for the grain."

(*Rebecca Ondov,* Great Horse Stories for Girls)

Wind Dancer learned to say thank you from her mom, Dancer.*

_____

_____

_____

_____

_____

_____

_____

_____

"The little girl's face turned sour, as if something was wrong. 'How do horses get clean if people don't give them bubble baths?'"

"I grinned. 'That's why God sends the rain—to wash the dirt away.'"

(*Rebecca Ondov*, Great Horse Stories for Girls)

Dazzle enjoying a bubble bath.*

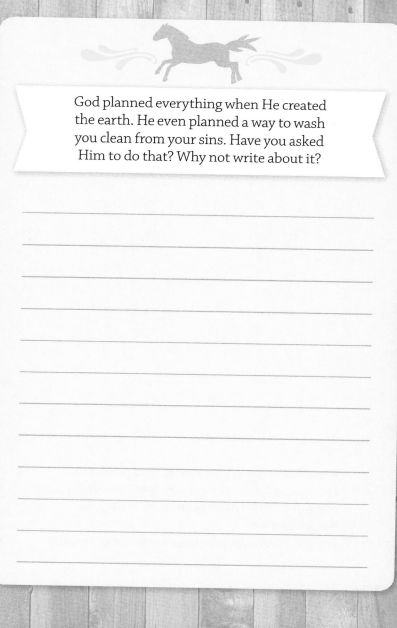

God planned everything when He created the earth. He even planned a way to wash you clean from your sins. Have you asked Him to do that? Why not write about it?

"A lone horse doesn't have the herd to protect them. Horses stay safe from mountain lions, grizzly bears, and wolves by staying in a group and facing the danger together."

(*Rebecca Ondov,* Great Horse Stories for Girls)

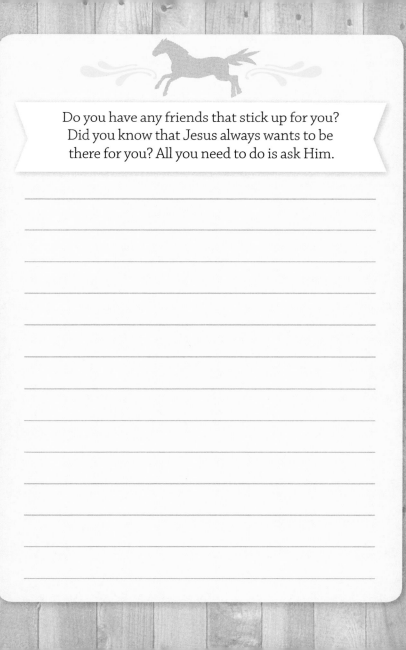

Do you have any friends that stick up for you?
Did you know that Jesus always wants to be
there for you? All you need to do is ask Him.

"Jesus replied: If anyone loves me, they will obey me. Then my Father will love them, and we will come to them and live in them" (John 14:23).

_____

_____

_____

_____

_____

_____

_____

_____

_____

_____

_____

_____

_____

"Above all, always remember that God loves you
with all His heart...and so do I."

(*Rebecca Ondov,* Great Horse Stories for Girls)

One More Thing...

Through horses I've learned so much about God. The biggest thing is how much He loves us. He wants each one of us to be a part of His family. Have you asked Him into your heart? If not, would you like to? Pray this prayer and believe it.

> Jesus, thank You for dying on the cross to pay for my sins. I've done some things that are wrong. I'm sorry. Please forgive me for all of them and wash my heart clean. I believe that You died on the cross for my sins, and You rose from the dead and are now living in heaven. I want You to be my Savior. Please come into my heart and change it—and me. Help me to trust You and follow You forever. Amen.

If you prayed this prayer with all your heart, welcome to God's family! Next, be sure to tell someone you know who believes in Jesus too. Then go to a church that teaches from the Bible and be baptized.

> "What are you waiting for? Get up! Be baptized, and wash away your sins by praying to the Lord" (Acts 22:16).

Join Rebecca Ondov for exciting horseback adventures!

Great Horse Stories for Girls!

Are You Crazy About Horses?

You love horses...and so does horsewoman Rebecca Ondov. She wants you to experience life around real horses—caring for them, getting to know their personalities, training them, and loving them. In these true stories you'll find out a lot about horses...and more about yourself, including how much God loves you. Discover how horses can help you

- create stronger friendships
- handle feelings, including discouragement
- believe in God's love and care
- make wiser choices
- live for God every day

Get ready to have a great time with Rebecca and her animals. You also may be surprised by how much God wants to talk to you, walk beside you, and be your friend.